ITALY

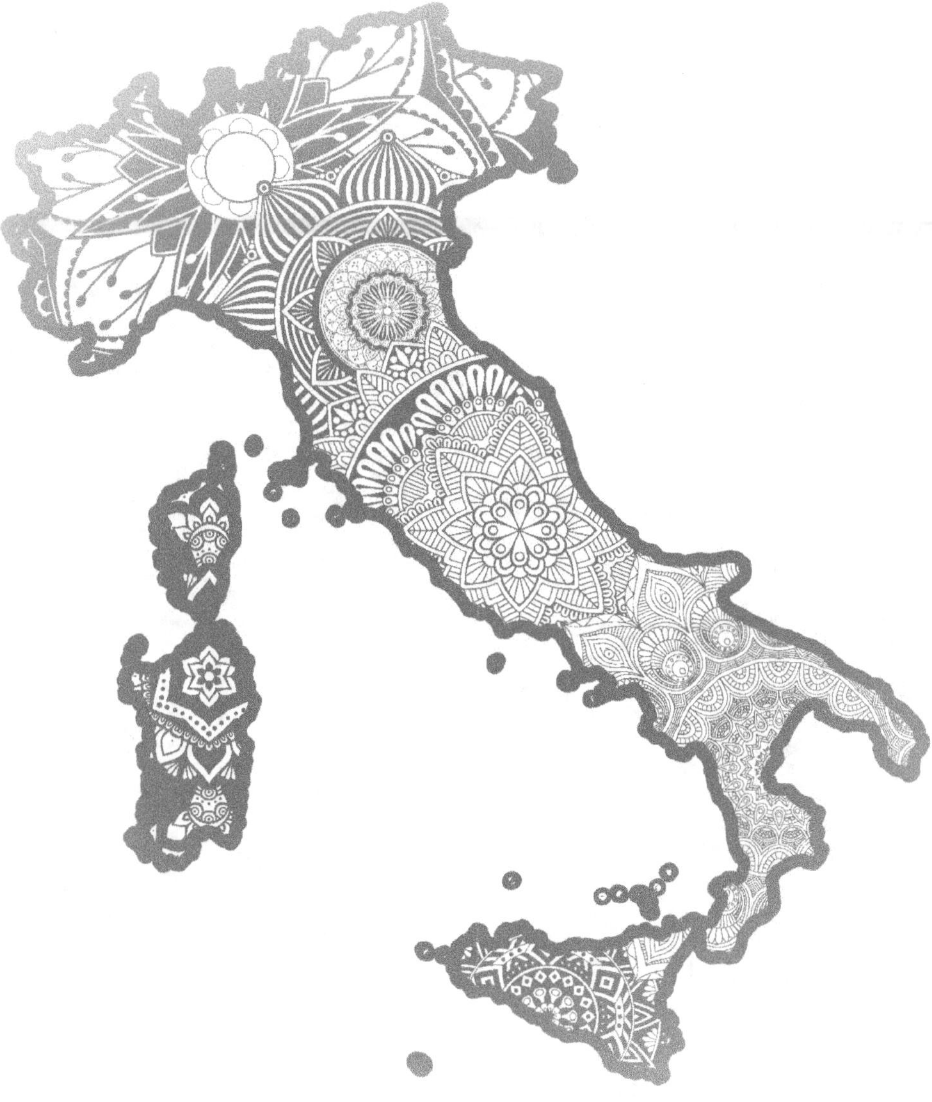

JORDAN

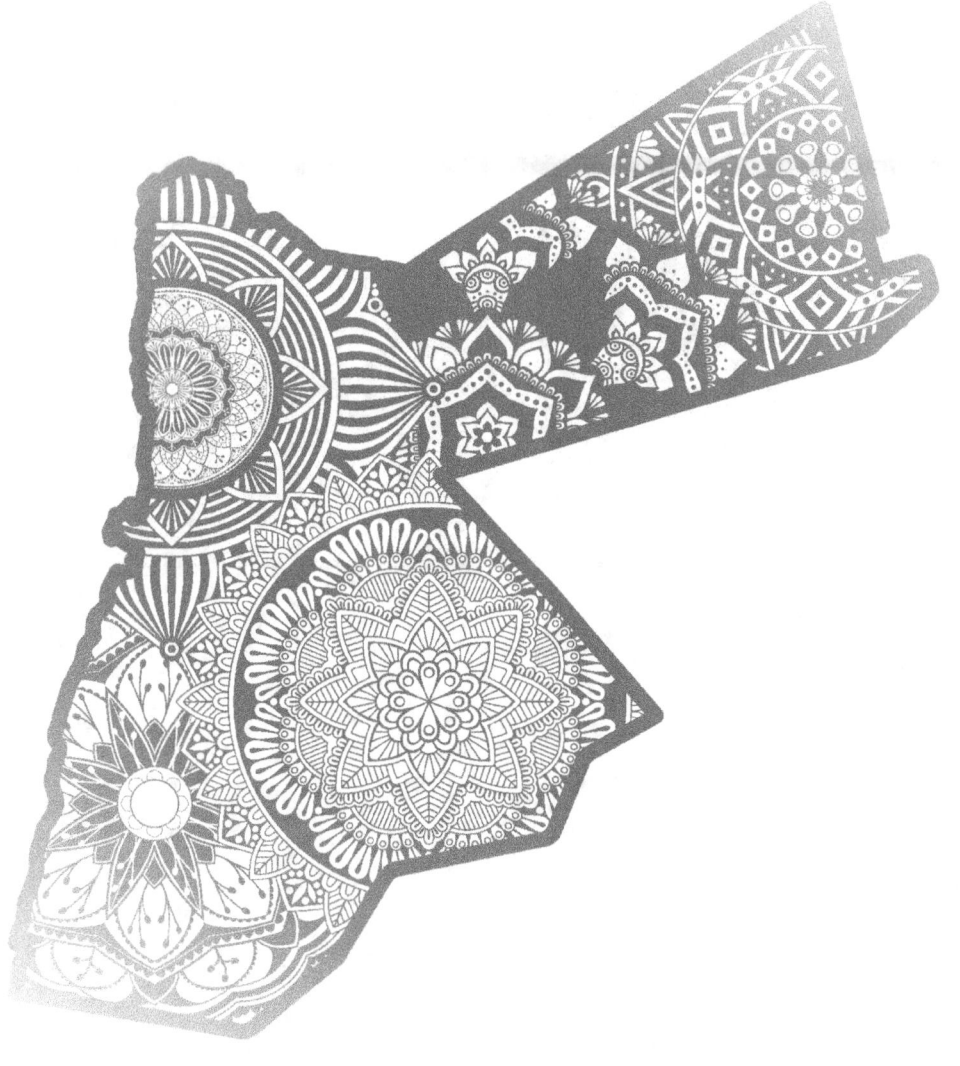

IRAN

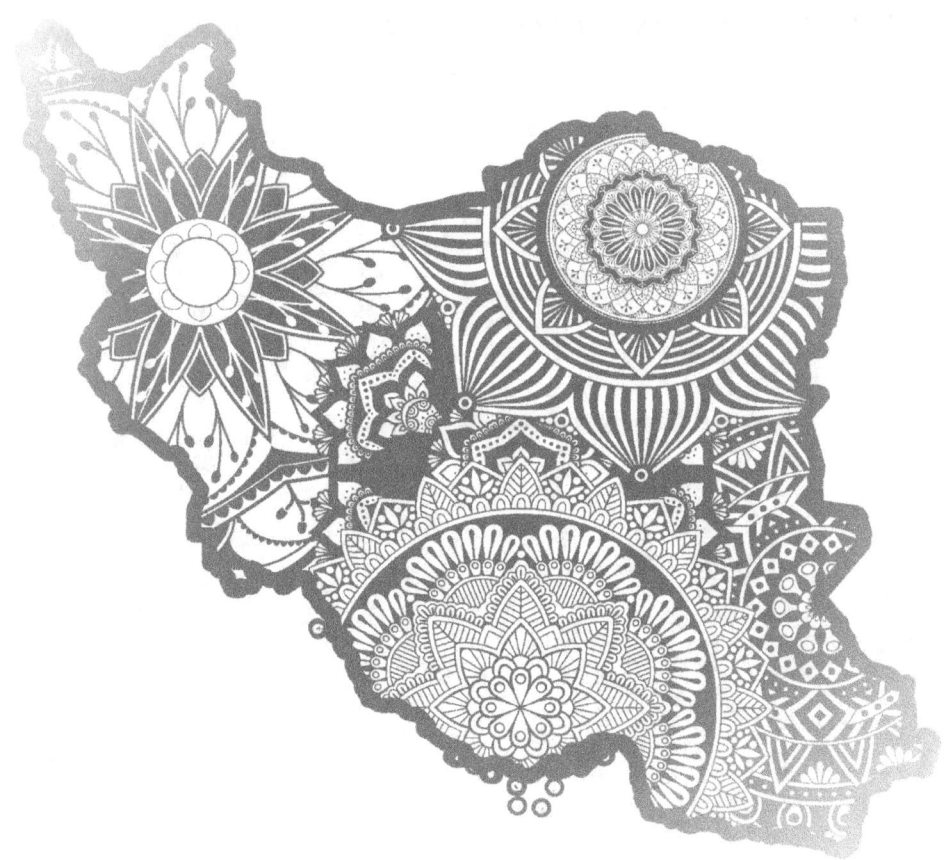

ANGOLA

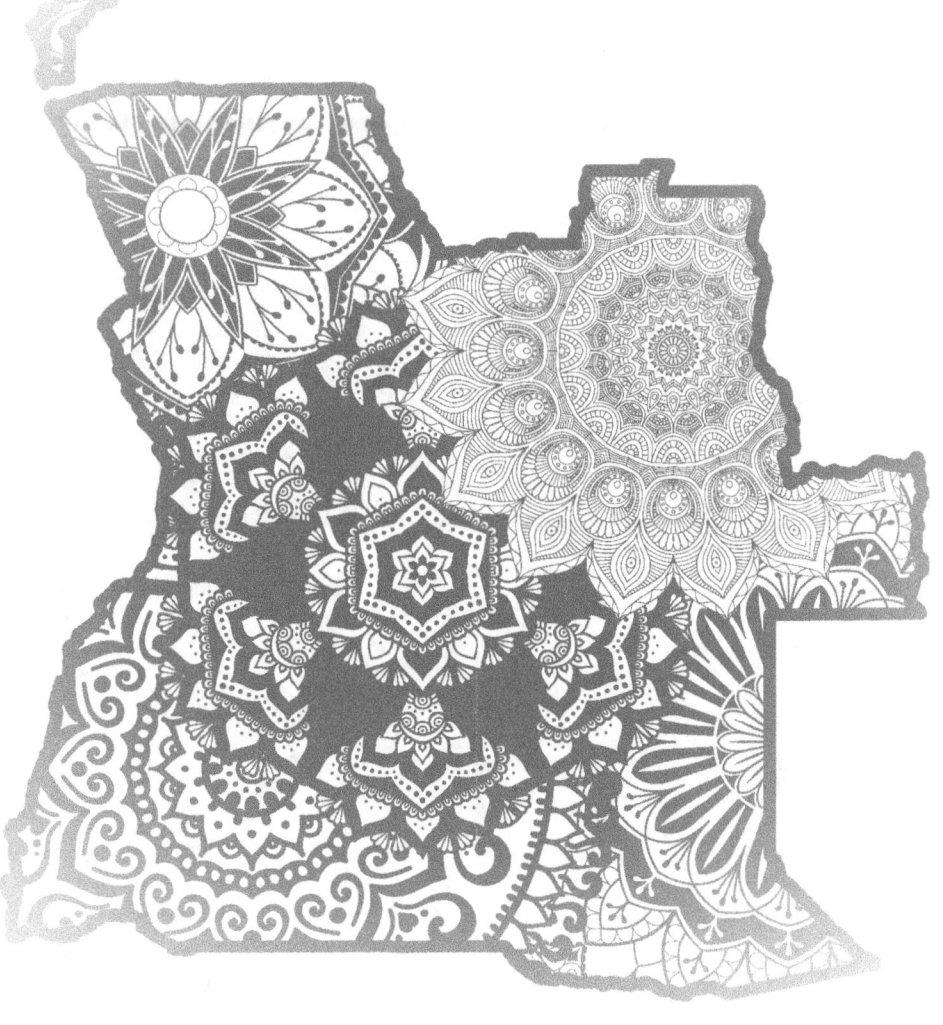

UNITED STATES OF AMERICA

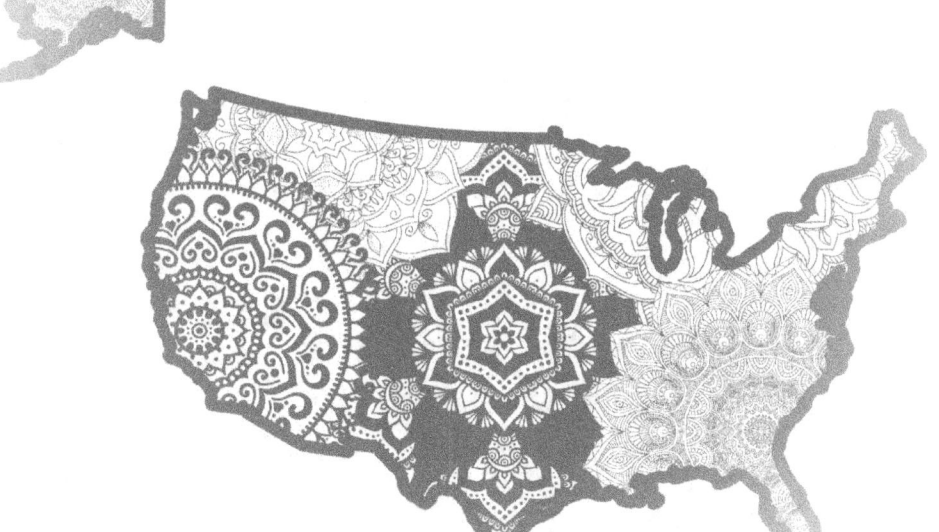

UGANDA

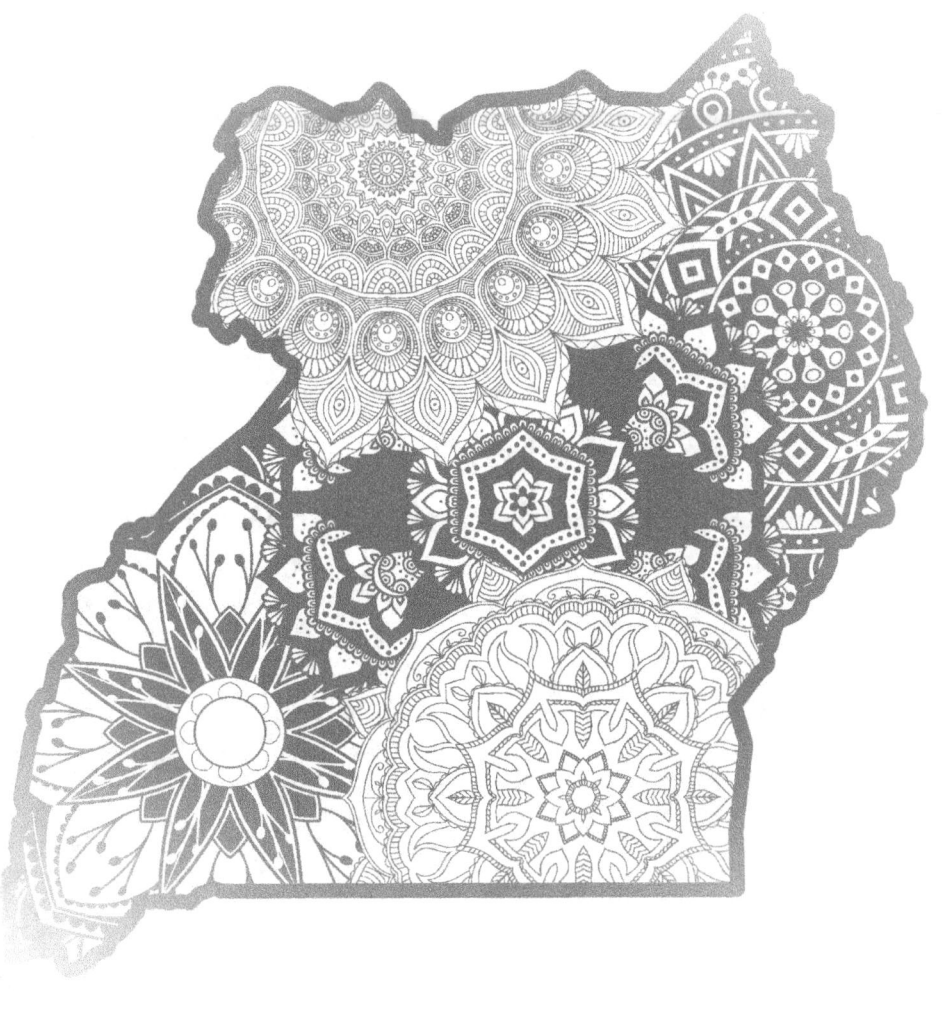

IRAQ

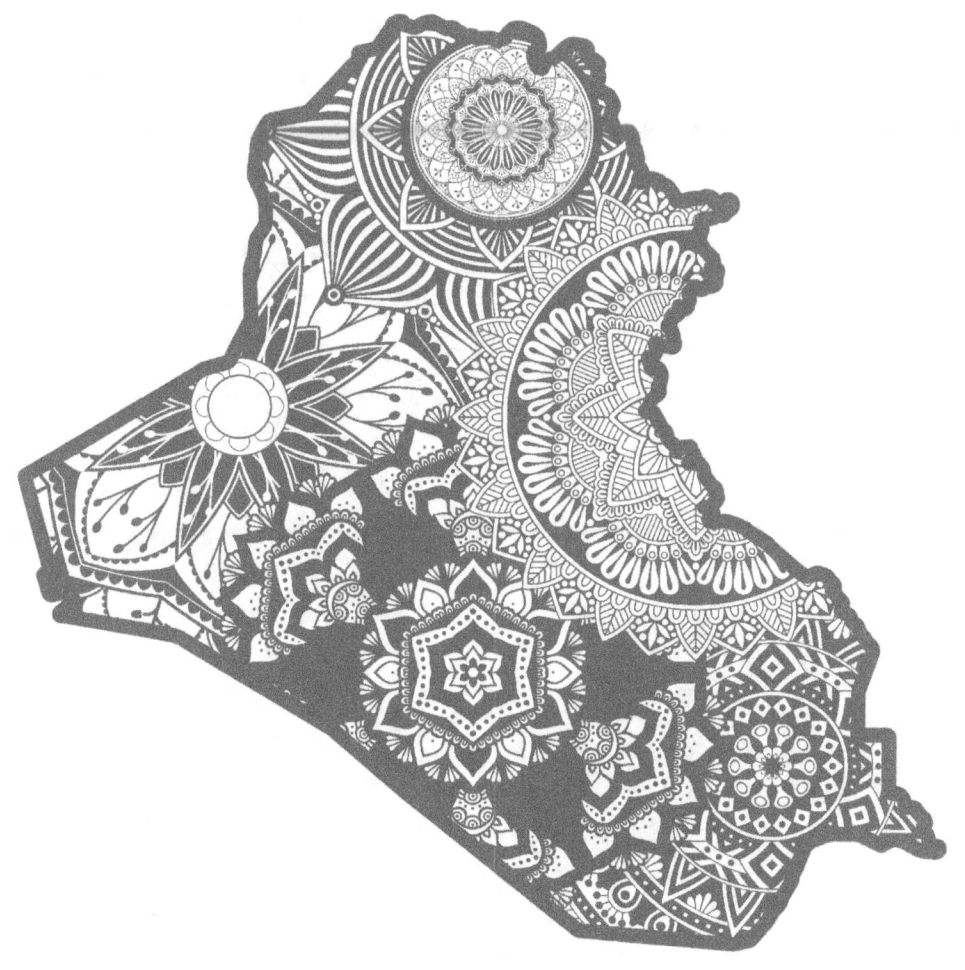

NIGERIA

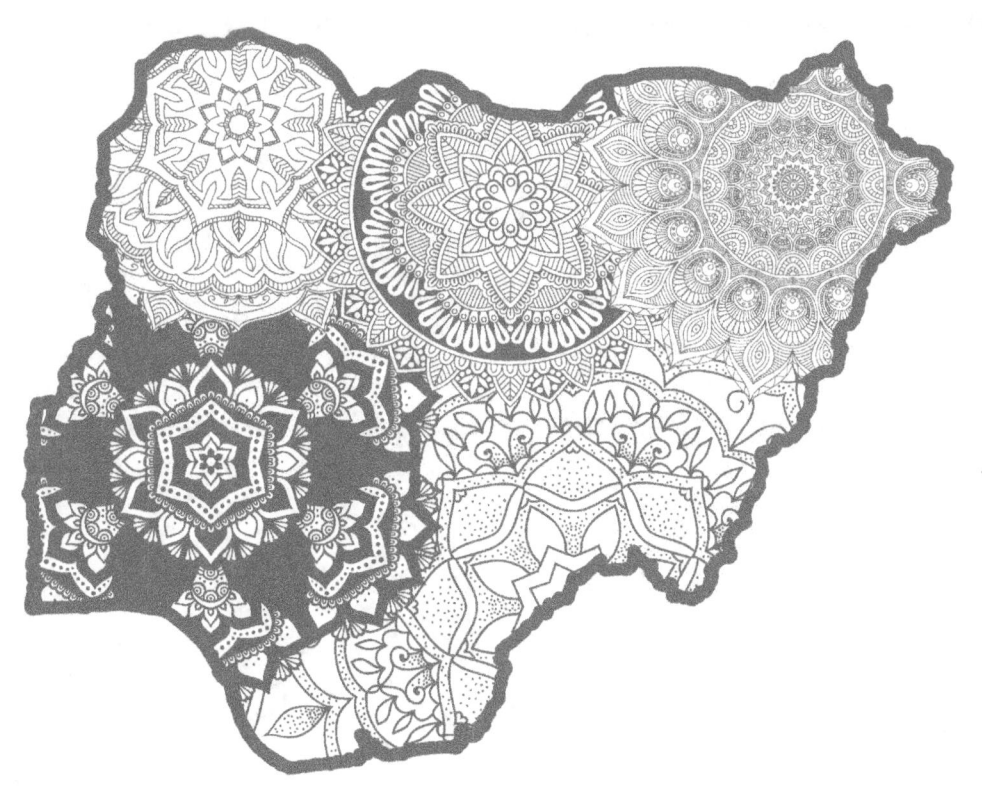

TANZANIA

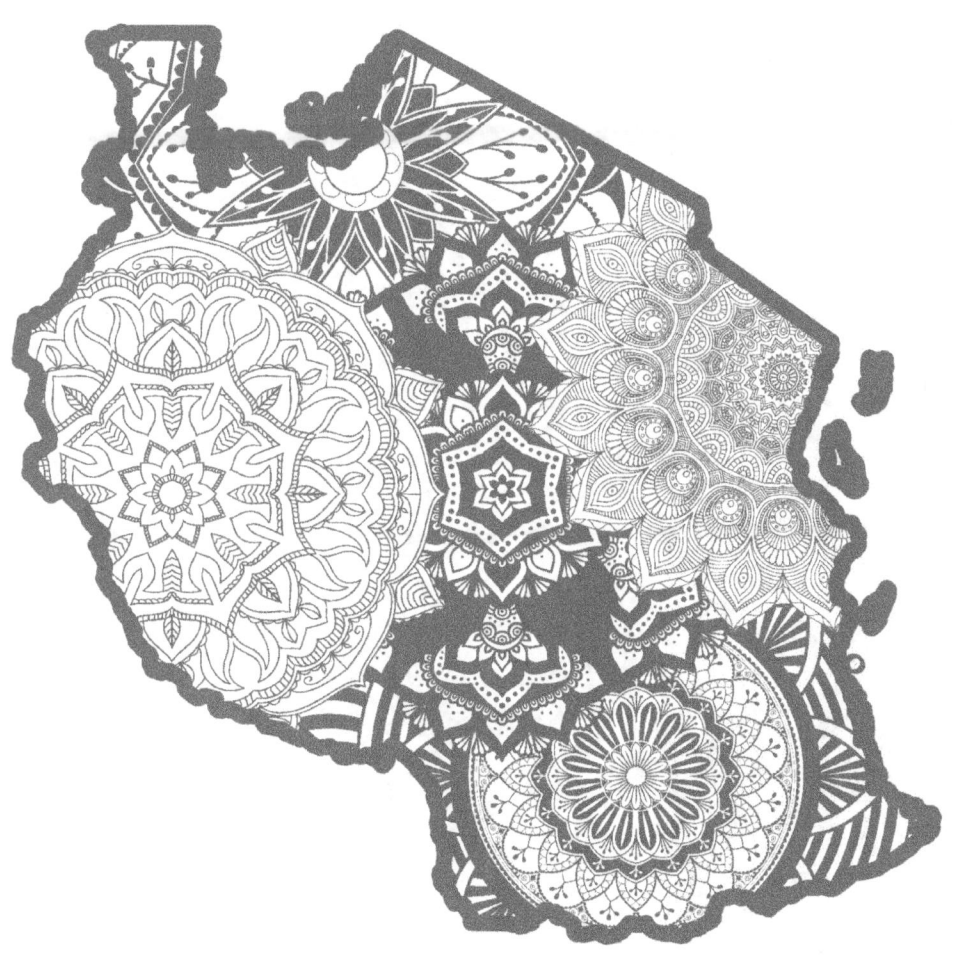

SWEDEN

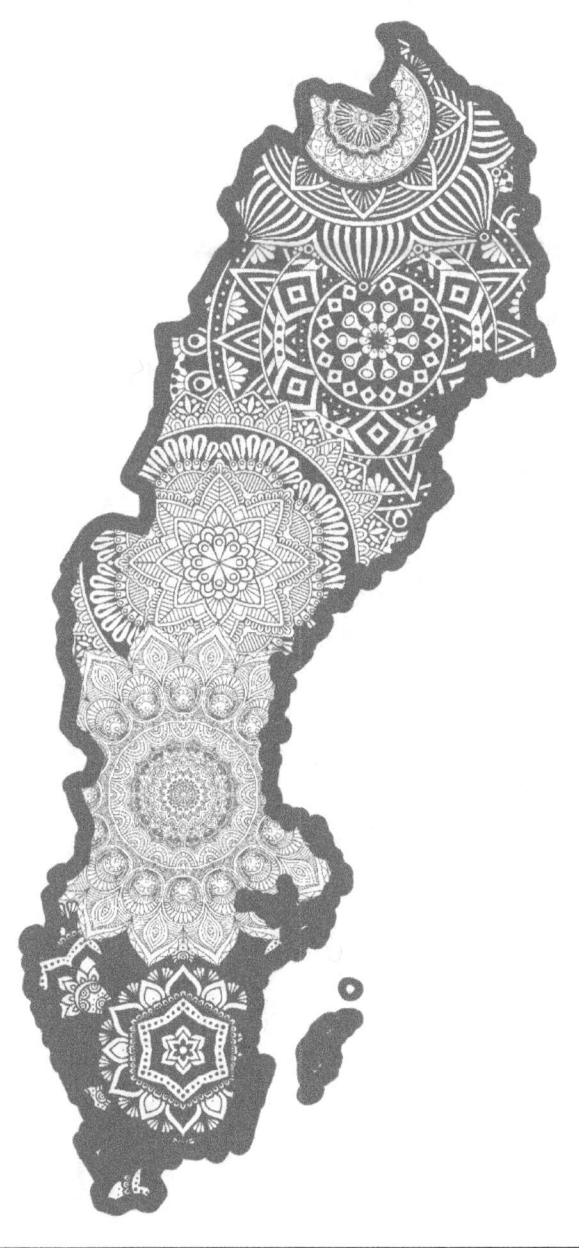

SYRIA

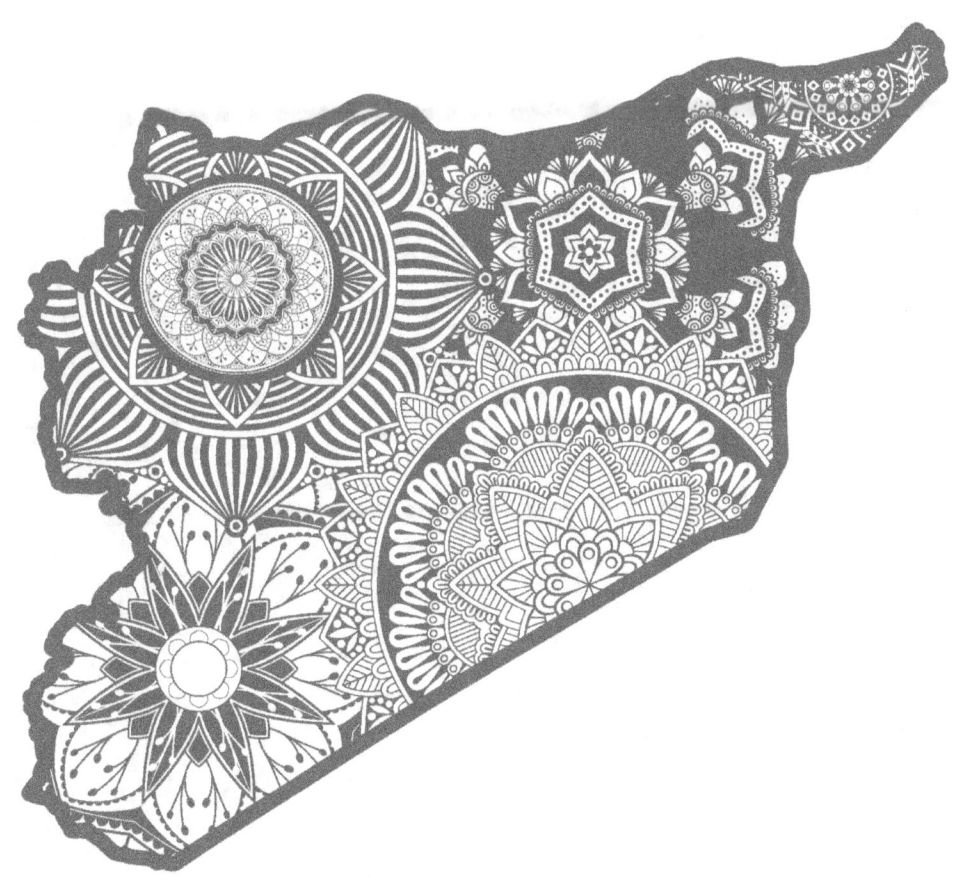

PERU

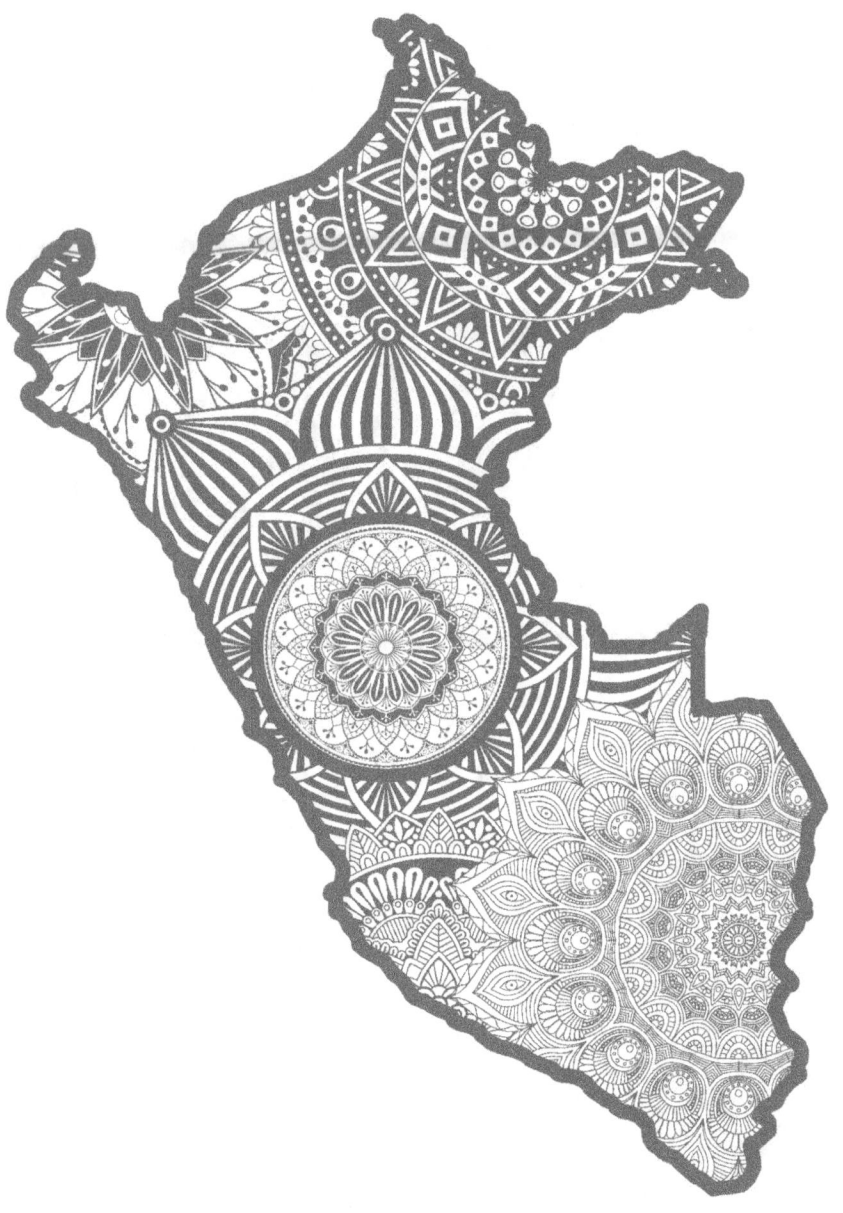

LIBYA

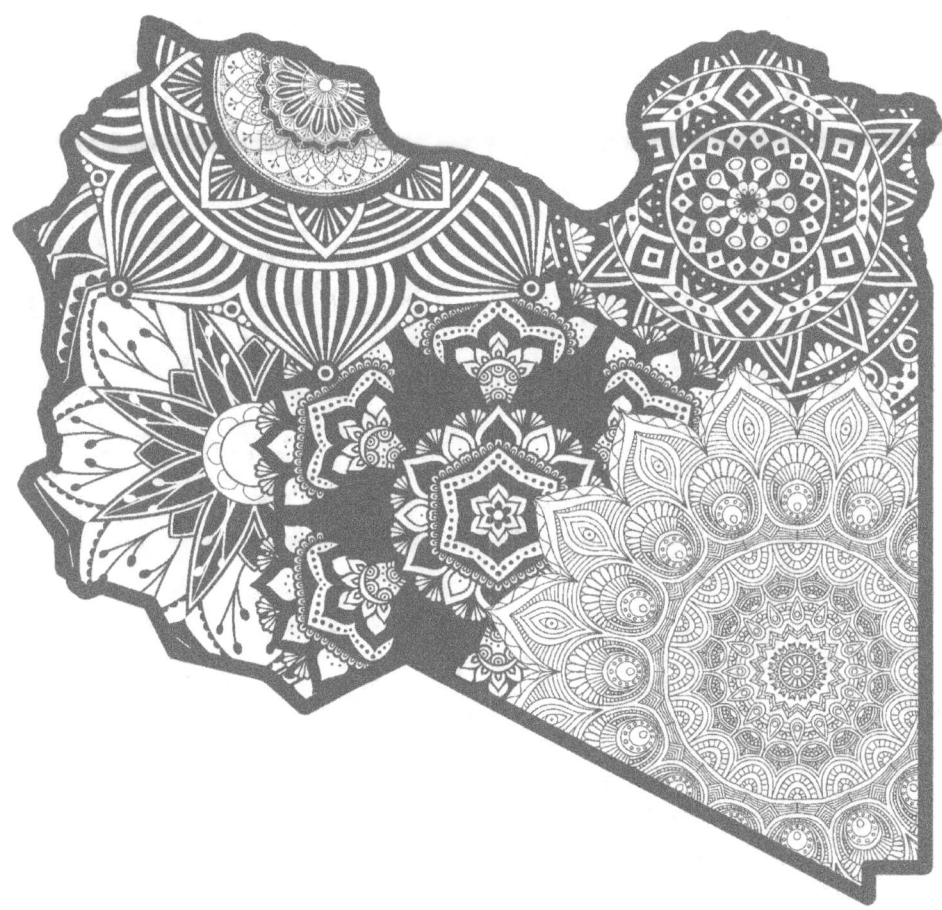

LAOS

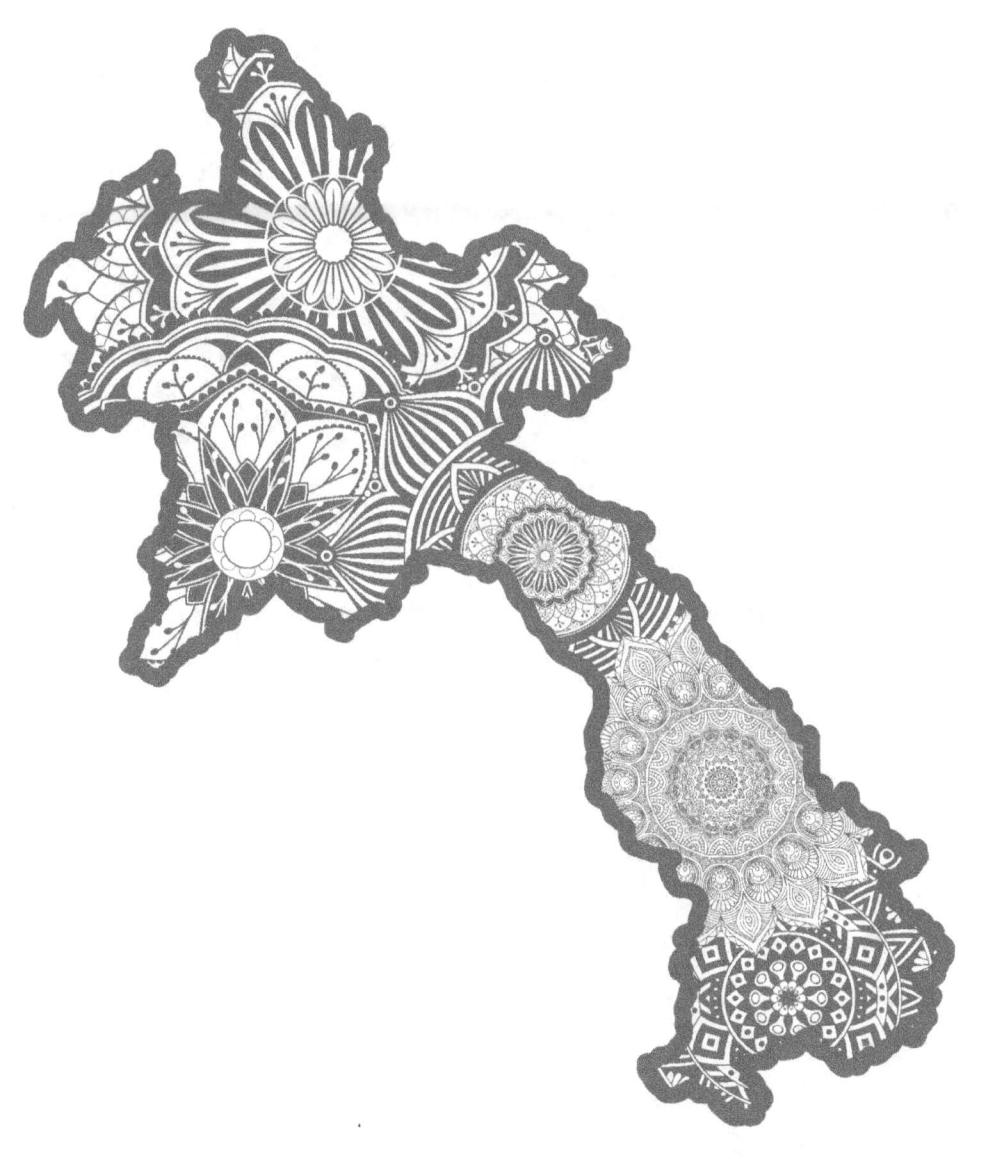

FRANCE

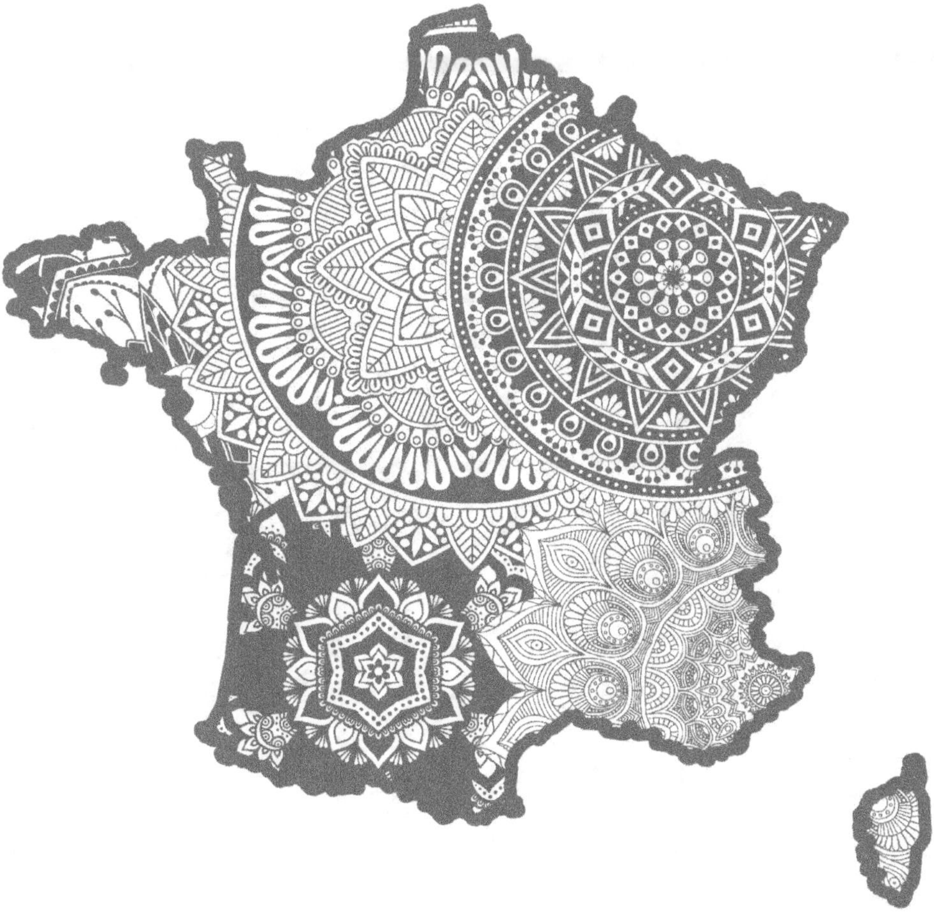

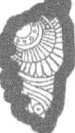

ARMENIA

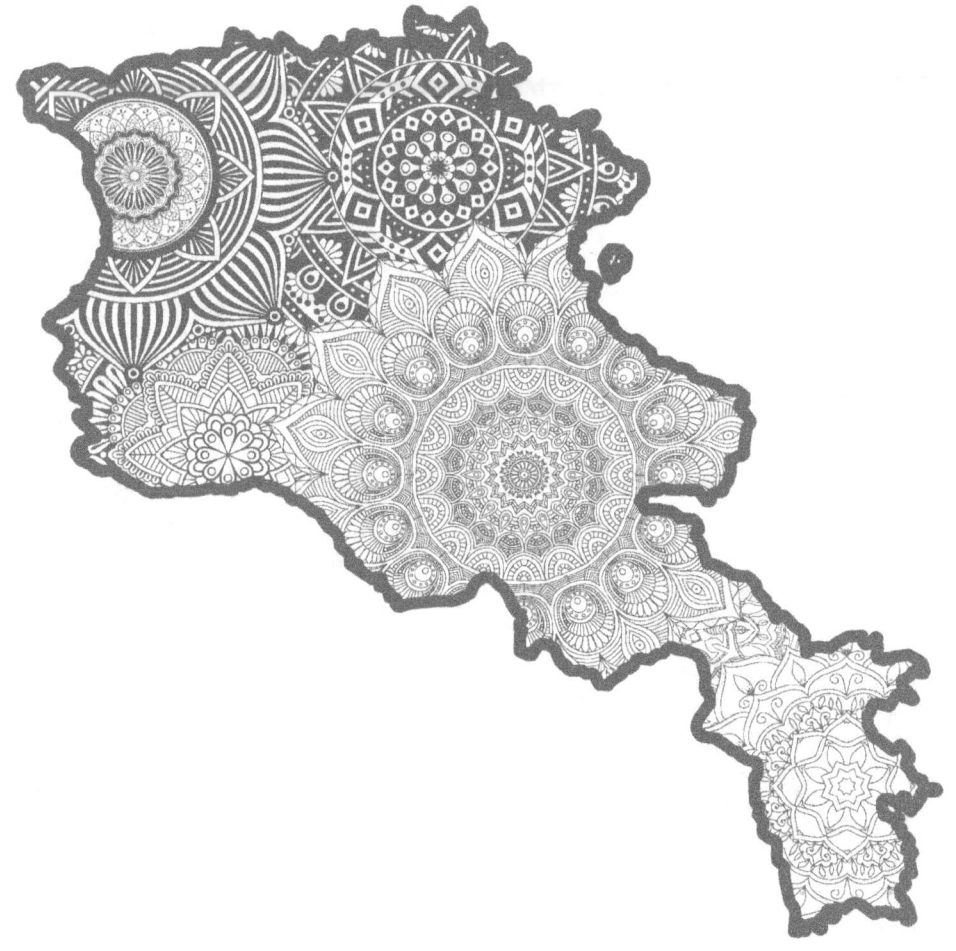

PORTUGAL

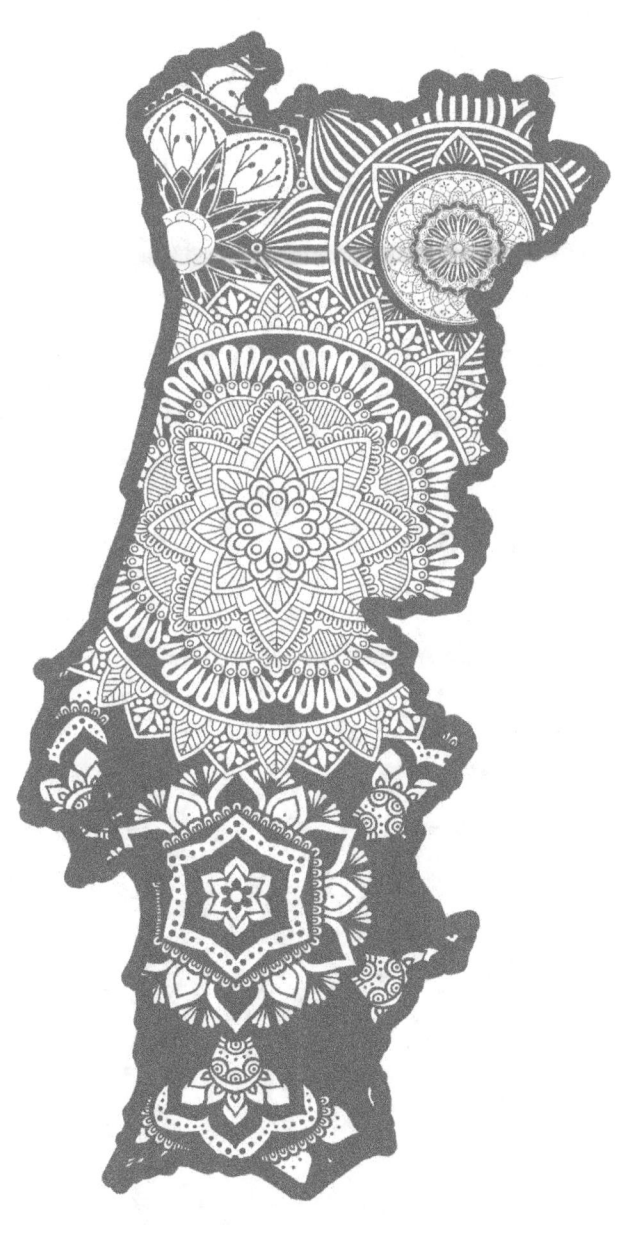

SERBIA

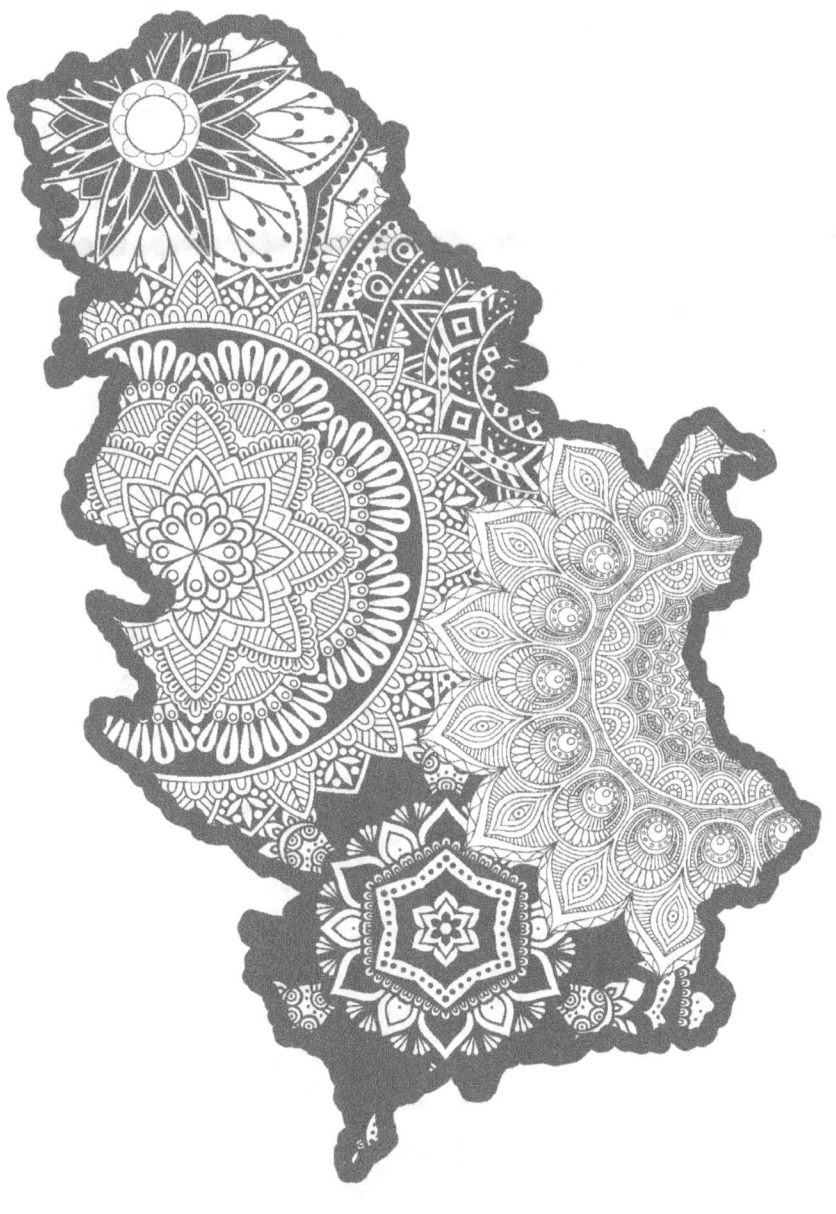

URUGUAY

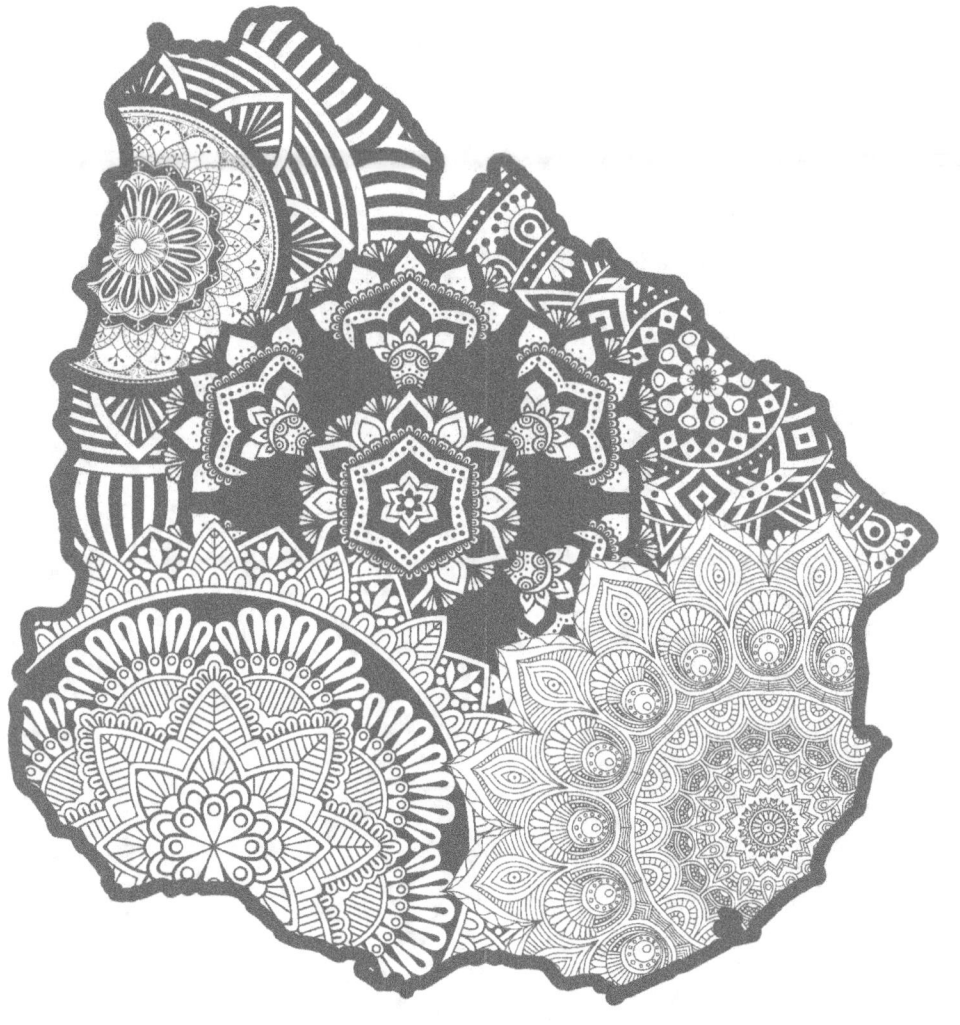

PAKISTAN

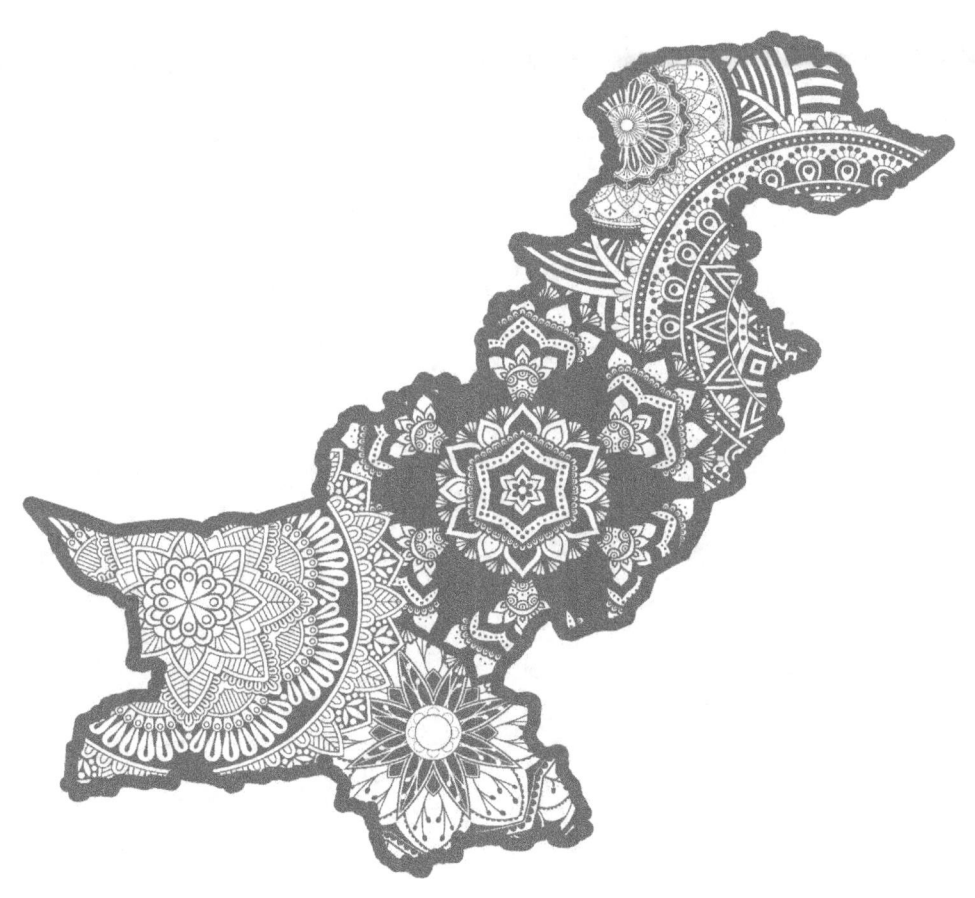

LEBANON

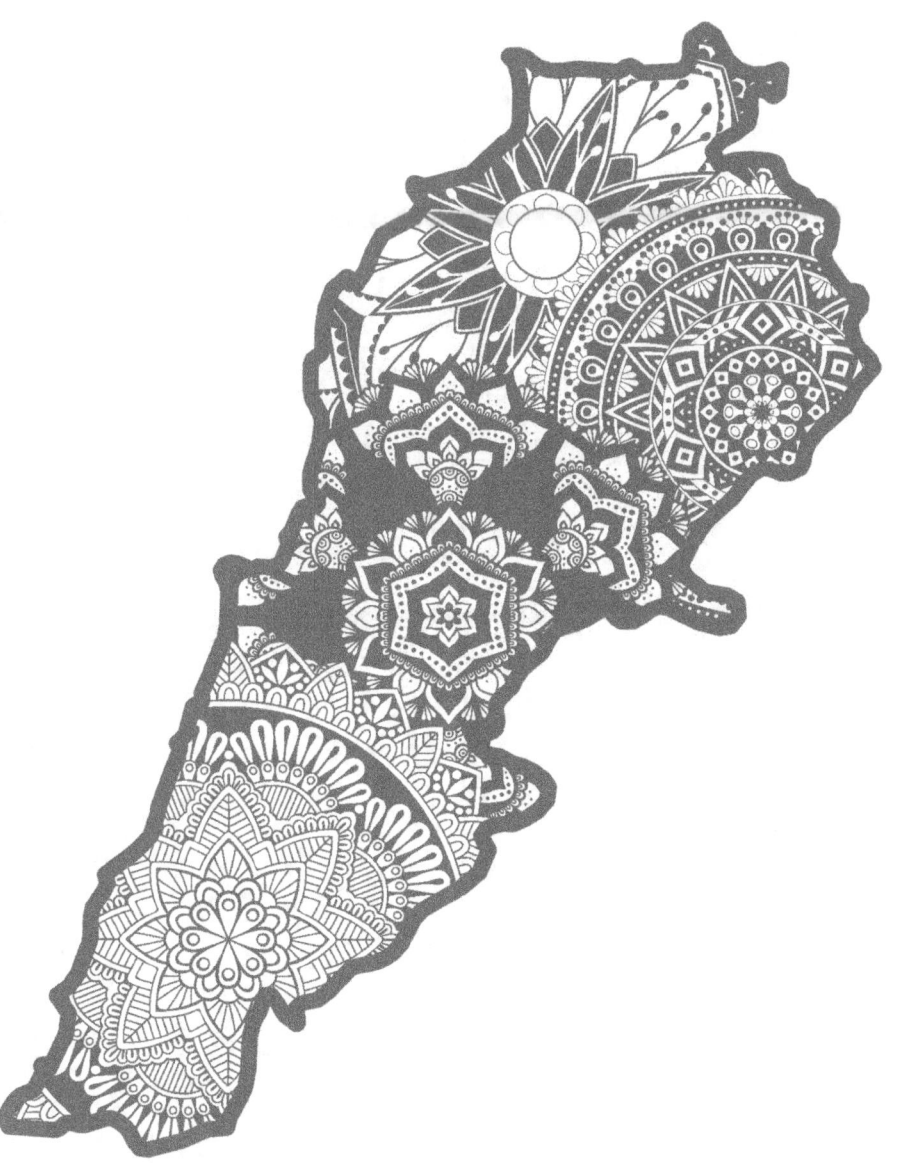

AUSTRALIA

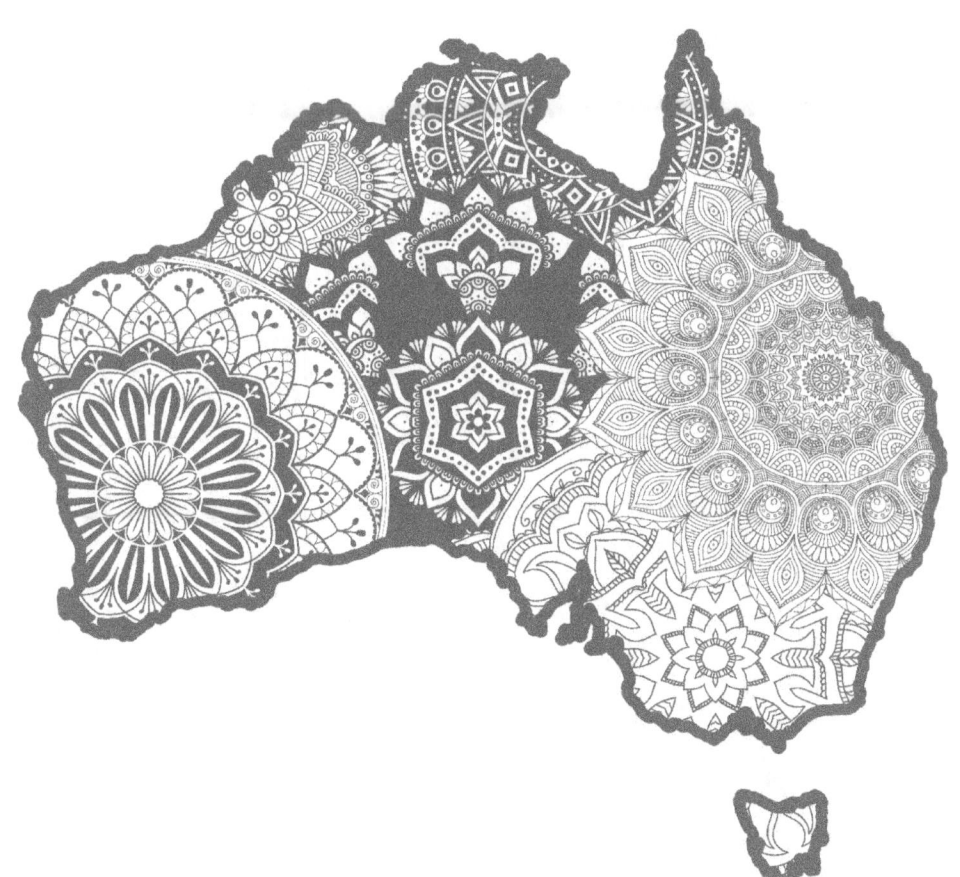

CONGO

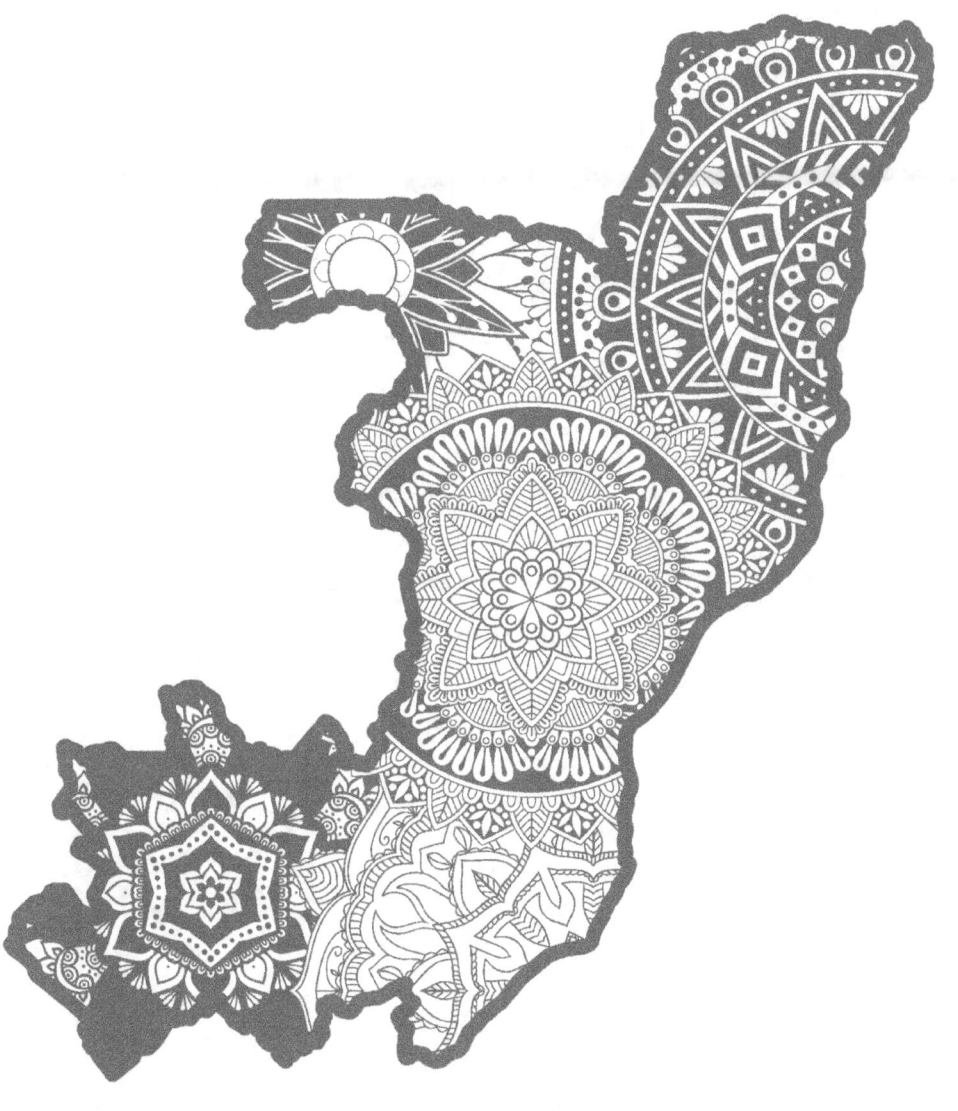

INDIA

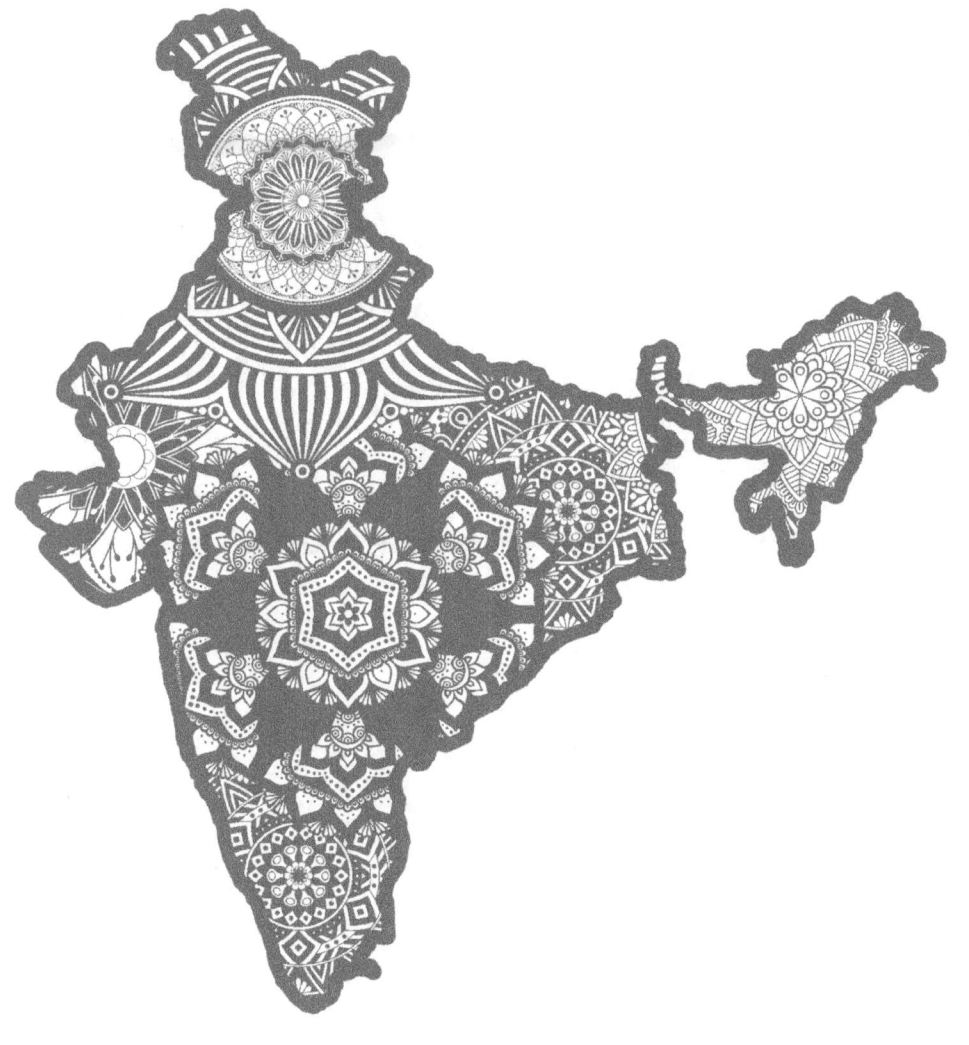

BARBADOS

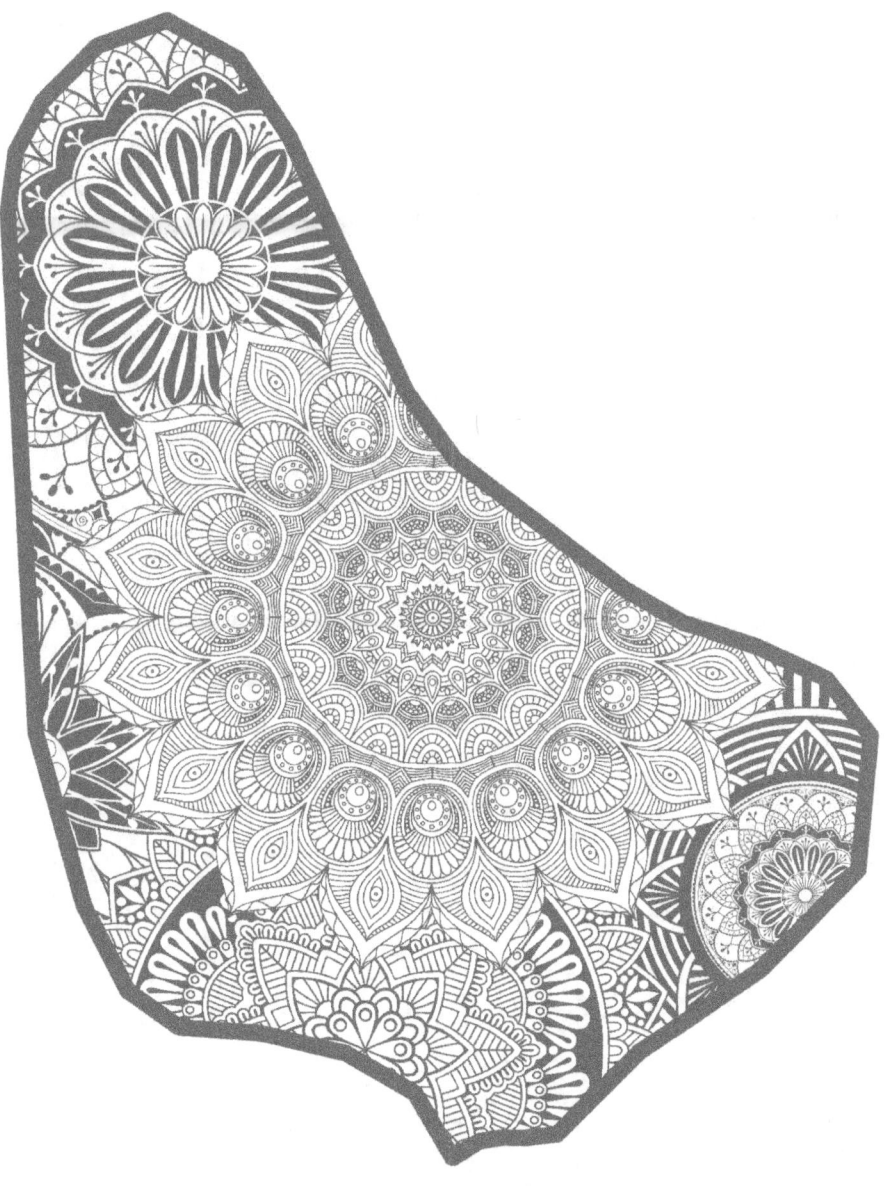

GERMANY

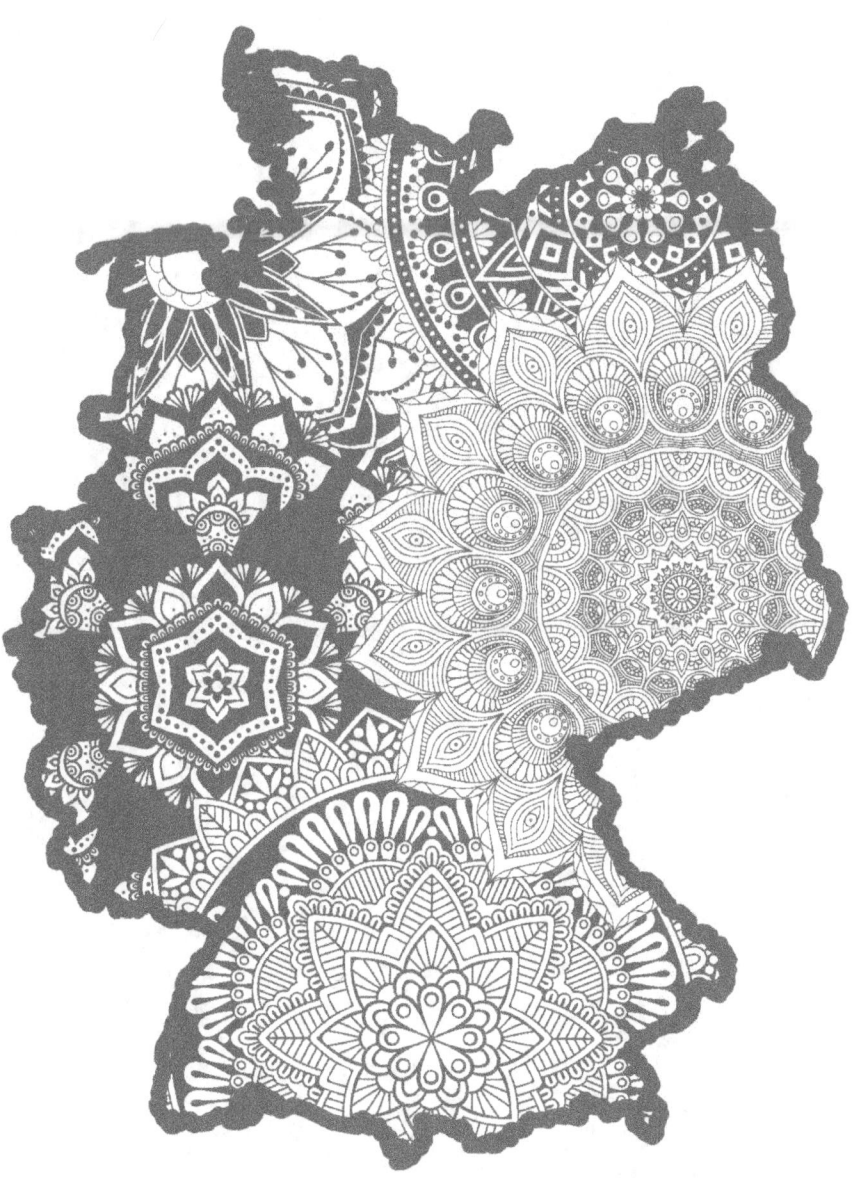

COLOMBIA

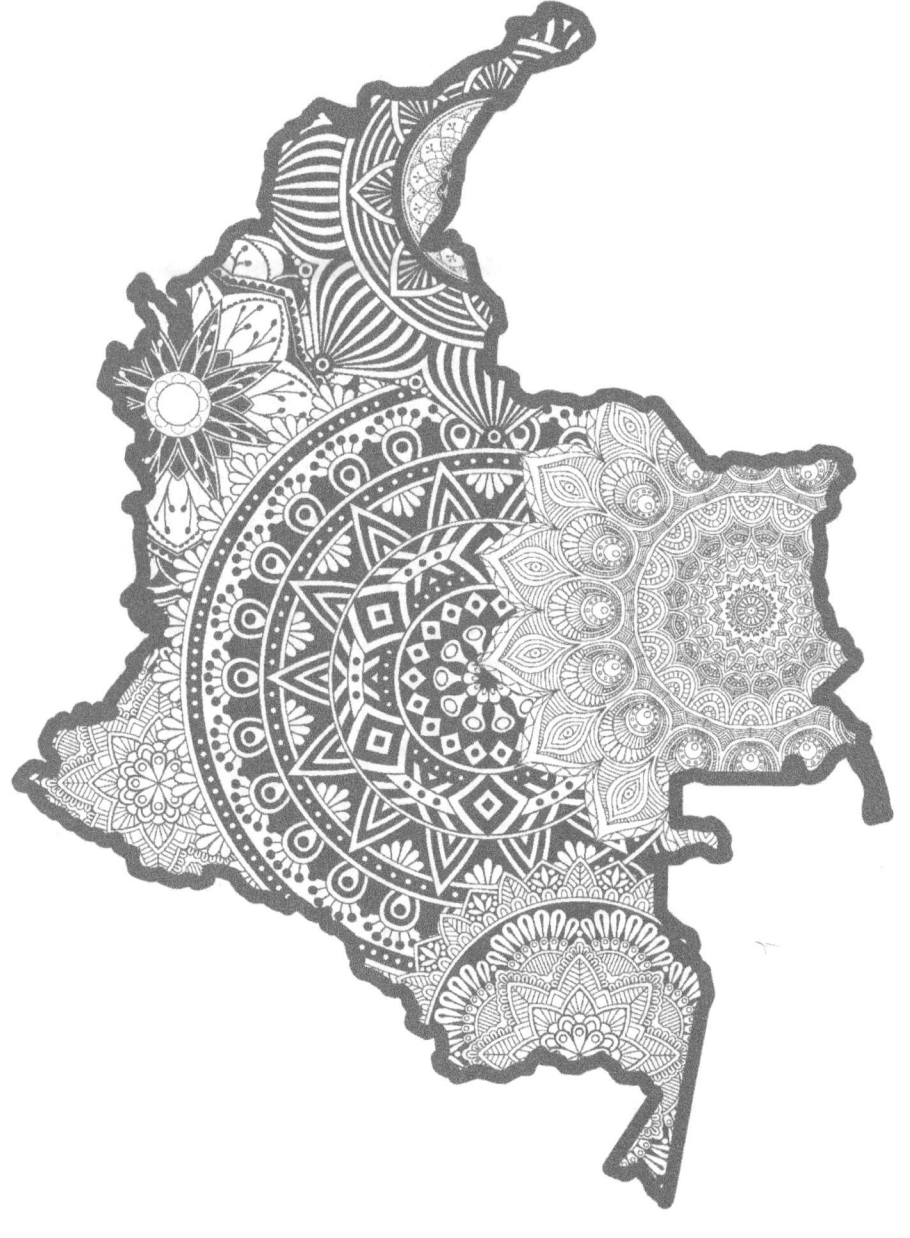

FINLAND

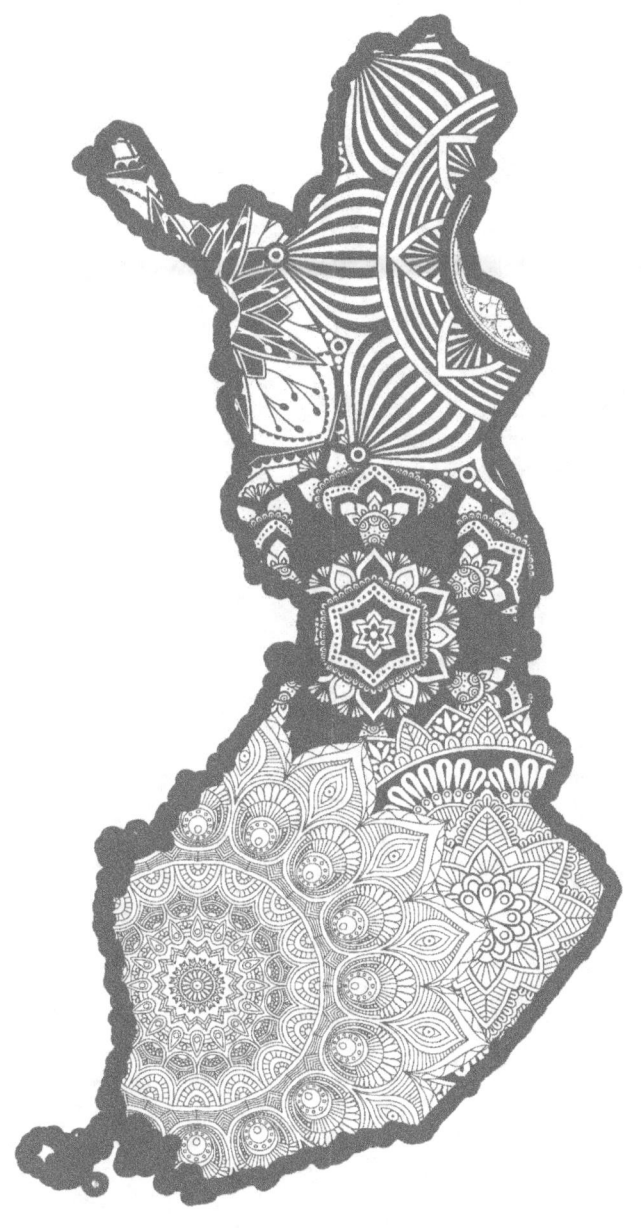

BELGIUM

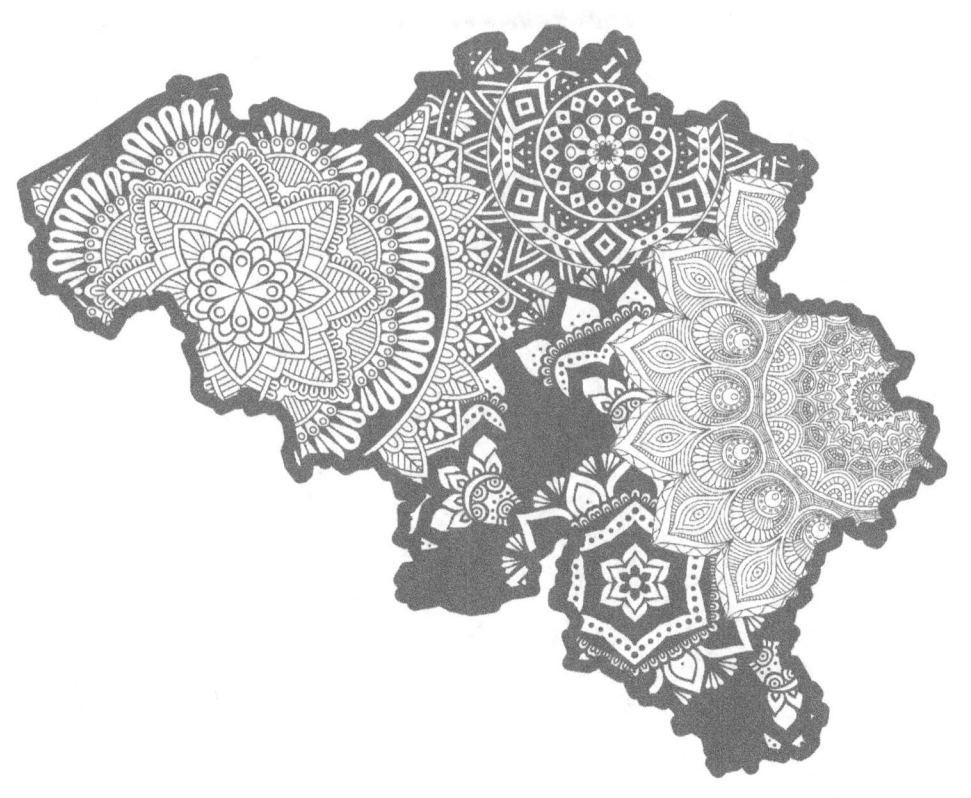

NORTH KOREA

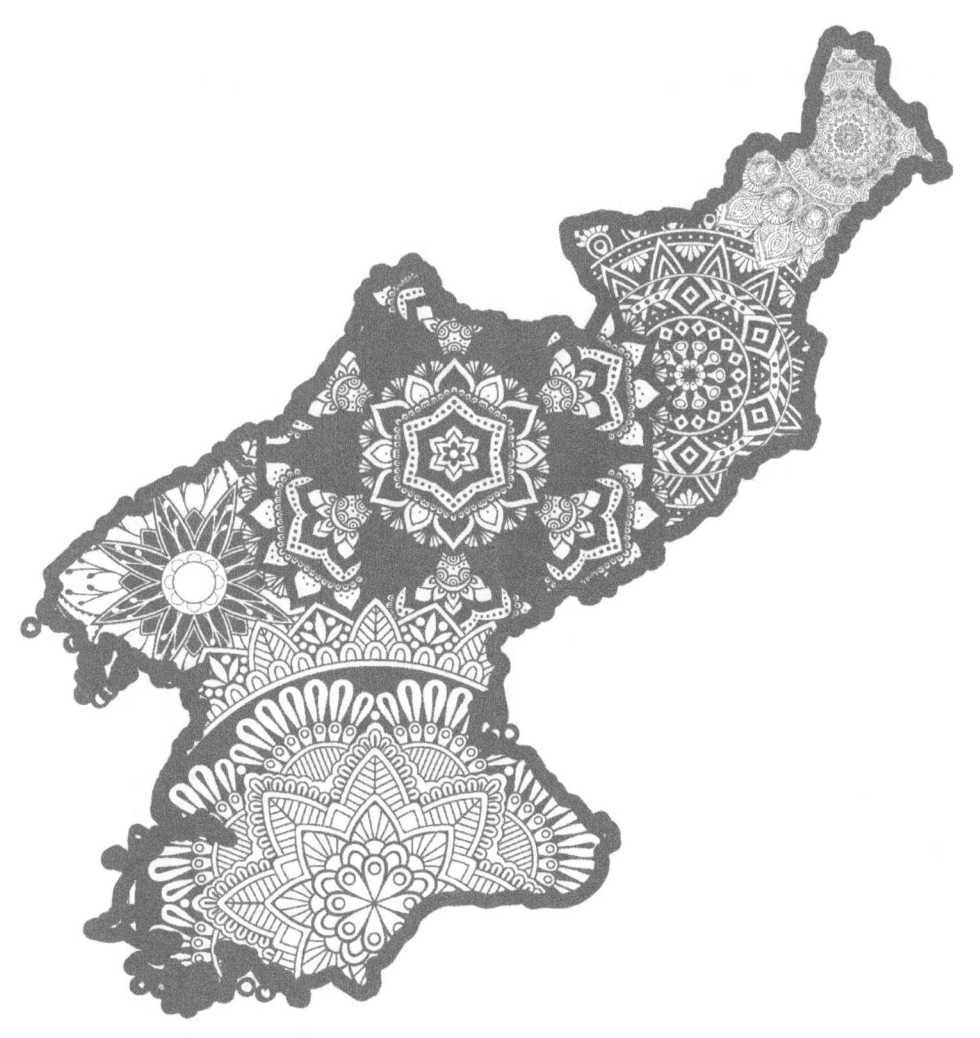

BRAZIL

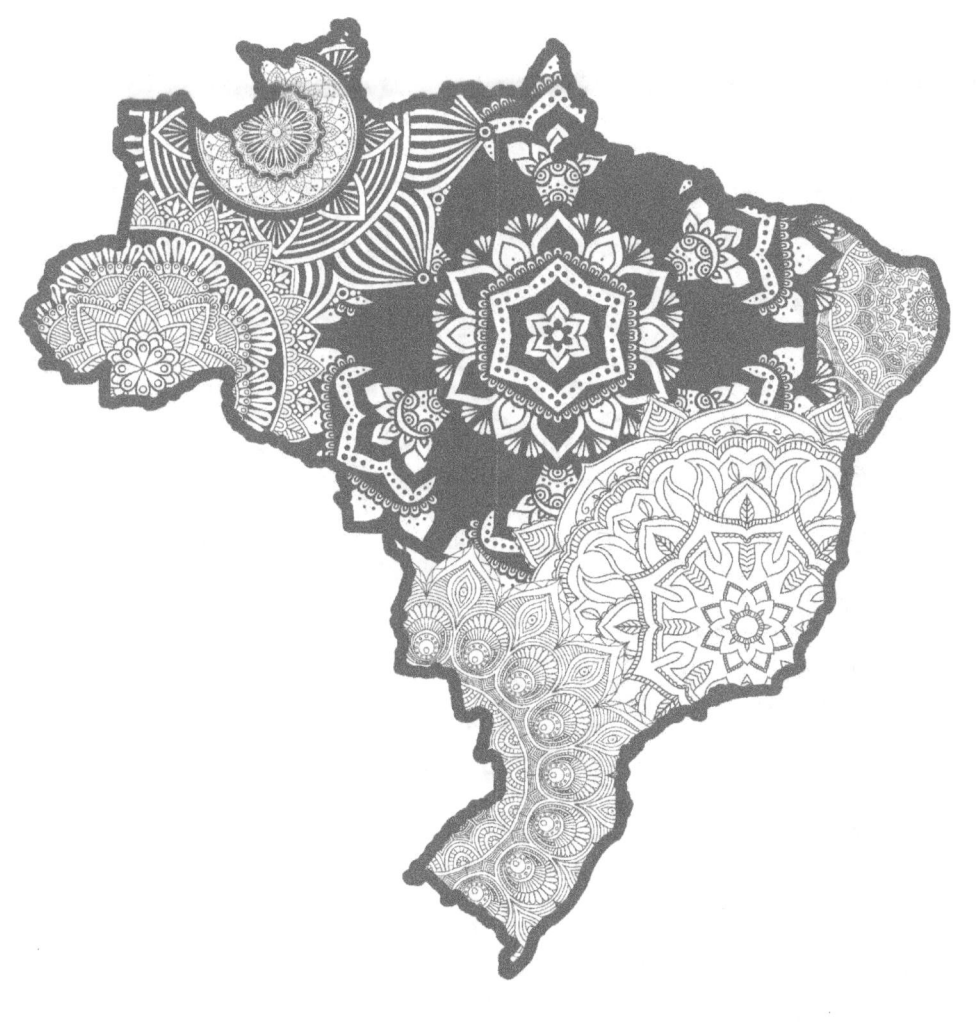